Of Trails and Towns

in the Black Hills and Badlands

Edith-Maria Redlin

ISBN-10: 1540523381

ISBN-13: 978-1540523389

Edith-Maria Redlin
4313 Portrush Rd.
Rapid City, SD 57702 USA
1 605 348-3890
edithmaria@rap.midco.net

DAKOTA TRAILS PRESS

Cover photo: Boulder Hill, Black Hills, South Dakota

Contents

Hay Camp at the Swift Waters

A long, long time ago, a river rushing down from the Black Hills cut into a ridge of sandstone foothills to the east. We call this sandstone ridge the "Hogback." The river carved out an opening about 1,500 feet wide, now known locally as the "Gap." The river still flowing through it is Rapid Creek.

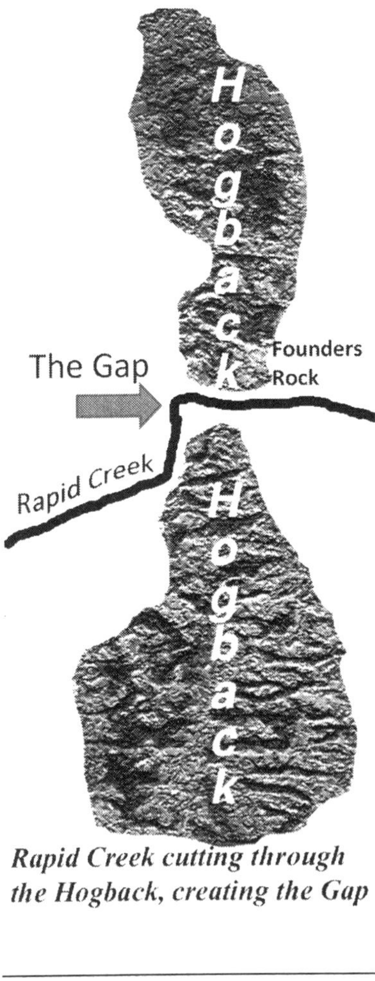

Rapid Creek cutting through the Hogback, creating the Gap

Long before white men came to the Black Hills, various native peoples had already lived here for about 7,000 years. There are indications that, when entering or leaving the Black Hills, Lakota and Cheyenne camped near Rapid Creek in the Gap of the Hogback below a rock formation now known as "Founders Rock."

They probably chose this spot because the rock and the Hogback behind it protected them from the cold northern wind. They carved pictures into the rock and performed rituals. This prehistoric Native American rock art, depicting among other things a deer and a human, can still be seen today.

Founders Rock

When you look at the above photo of Founders Rock, you probably assume that it is tucked away somewhere in the Black Hills, surrounded by pine trees and mountains. But I actually had a hard time taking this picture because that Tuesday, at 11:00 a.m., an unceasing stream of cars, trucks and busses went by on Omaha Street, just below Founders Rock, which is situated in the heart of Rapid City. I had to wait some time to get a picture undisturbed by traffic.

When you examine the left half of the rock face, you see some faint black letters, and you wonder if they stem from long ago or if they consist of wiped-off graffiti from our days? To me, they seem to announce some event or to advertise a business. The upper line seems to spell "MIRHENDA" or something of the sort. Maybe some time ago a clever businessman used the rock as a billboard.

This rock has had a lot of human attention through the ages. At first Native Americans came here, then the white people. One of the first whites was John Brennan. In 1876, he had been looking for gold in the Palmer Gulch area, but was disappointed because he did not find any and came down from the Hills into the open grasslands along Rapid Creek.

View from Founders Rock down to Rapid Creek and over to the Black Hills

With eleven other men, including a surveyor named Samuel Scott, Brennan set up camp on February 25, 1876, right below Founders Rock near the creek. Isn't it amazing that we know the exact date, 140 years ago, when these men camped here? To us, 140 years seems like a long time span, but when I consider that my own grandmothers were born in 1874 and 1876, I realize that this was only two generations away. Can you imagine that one of my grandmothers was already two years old when John Brennan and his group camped at Founders Rock, and my other grandmother was born just a few days afterwards, on March 10 of 1876?

It looked quite different here in 1876 than it looks today. There was nothing man-made around; it was an unknown land to the white people. Brennan saw nothing but grass and cottonwood trees along the river. Only the rocks looked similar to what we see now.

It might have been a cold night, that February 25, 1876, and maybe they put up their tents in the snow. But they seemed to like the location because they started talking about staying here. Rather than search for gold, why not provide a hay camp here to supply all the people coming through?

According to John Brennan's journal, he already had the intention to lay out a townsite somewhere in the foothills when he came down from Palmer Gulch, and that night this new idea was discussed at the campfire. The twelve men decided then and there to set up a town called "Rapid City," named for the fast running water of the creek that still cuts right through it and can become quite "rapid" in the spring after the snow melt. The Lakota name for Rapid City is "Minniluzahan", meaning "Swift Water."

Brennan might have sensed the historic significance of this decision when he carved his last name into the sandstone cliff. The name can still to be seen today, but it is gradually getting fainter.

Where is the most logical place to set up a town? Well, a flat surface near some running water would be the preferred spot. That's what our founding fathers of Rapid City realized, too. The next morning, they went to work and laid out the townsite under the direction of the surveyor Samuel Scott. They walked or rode down along Rapid Creek for about 2,500 feet to the east and chose a place where its swift waters ran through. There, not far from where they camped, they found a square mile that was quite flat.

With his compass in hand, Samuel Scott laid out the town as a square which reached exactly one mile from west to east—from West Boulevard to East Boulevard—and one mile from north to south—from North Street to South Street. There is a curious detail about this original square mile: When you see it on the map, you notice that it is tilted to the east. The town fathers did not take into account that magnetic north deviates about eleven degrees to the east of true north at this spot.

I find it remarkable that these men bothered to measure out a full square mile. With all the land available to them in 1876, wouldn't you think that a town could just be an accumulation of sod houses, huts, sheds, stores and stables, sprouting up from places that the pioneers choose haphazardly? But our founding fathers were more orderly. Thus the original square mile was laid out just east of the Hogback, and to our day, 140 years later, it still contains the center of the city.

The original square mile of Rapid City a.k.a. Hay Camp

Although the layout was not oriented to true north, nobody minded this little error, and the twelve men started building their huts in the new town. It turned out to be a good idea to establish themselves in this region where many pioneers and miners came through, needing not only hay for horses, mules and oxen, but all kinds of tools, wood, food, clothing, etc.

Merchants and their families started building their houses and shops in the new settlement. Cattle drivers and freighters—men who shipped goods by wagon across the western plains—had their camps on Rapid Creek. They needed lots of hay to feed their animals and nicknamed the new town "Hay Camp." Hay Camp quickly became the gateway to the Black Hills.

By the summer of 1876, two hundred people already populated the new settlement. Were they not aware that it was illegal for white people to live here? According to the Fort Laramie Treaty of 1868, this was the Great Sioux Reservation, and all the land belonged to the Lakota. Hay Camp was raided several times, causing the majority of the settlers to give up and move back east to Fort Pierre.

Only nineteen of them stayed. One of them was Rufus "Pap" Madison. An old drawing of the town shows only seventeen buildings. One of them, the Pap Madison cabin, is the oldest structure in Rapid City, built in the center of the original town site in February of 1876 on the corner of Fifth and Rapid Street.

He used hand-hewn cottonwood logs from trees right there at Rapid Creek to build the cabin. To insulate it from cold and water, Madison pushed grass, moss, sticks and wood chips into the cracks between the logs and then sealed everything with mud. The cabin had a dirt floor and measured only fifteen by fifteen feet, just enough for a bachelor like Pap Madison.

The restored historic "Pap" Madison cabin, now standing at the Journey Museum

In those early days, only a little wood-burning cookstove heated the cabin. This was actually more efficient than the fireplace which was added much later, in 1927, and made from local limestone quarried at nearby Lime Creek.

Interior of the restored Pap Madison Cabin (Photo Courtesy of the Minnilusa Historical Association in Rapid City)

Just like all the others at Hay Camp, Madison was not from this area. Born in New York State in 1832, he was a Yankee, a native of New England. Until 1870, he worked as a laborer in the region where he was born. For some unknown reason, he then moved far away, to Kansas.

From there, it was not such a big step anymore to follow the gold rush to the Black Hills in 1876. I don't know if he ever tried to find some gold or if he had any luck in finding it. But he did not live very long in this most famous, very first cabin of Rapid City. In 1878, Madison moved to Rapid Valley to become a farmer, only coming to town from time to time to sell his produce.

In the late 1880s, railroads from the south and from the east reached Rapid City. When the first train made it up from Nebraska in 1886, no more freighters and cattle drivers were around and the name "Hay Camp" disappeared.

In 1900, the first sawmill was established in Rapid City. Now progress could not be stopped, and Rapid City developed into an important regional trade center. During all of these years, Madison continued farming his 160 acres in the Valley until he left for Washington State in 1892 and was never seen in Rapid City again.

His cabin, however, survived. It was acquired by John Brennan who used it as a barn for many years. It probably would have deteriorated by now if the Fortnightly Club, a group of prominent women in Rapid City, had not restored it in 1927 after moving it to Halley Park, which is located in the Gap right outside of the original townsite, about 2,000 feet away from Founders Rock.

In 1928, the cabin became Rapid City's first historical museum. As a museum of 225 square feet was not adequate in the long run, the museum moved out again. For a while, the cabin was vacant or served as storage for lawn care equipment. For 86 years, it stood in the same place in Halley Park until its second move in 2012.

Now the cabin stands in front of the Journey Museum and has been restored to the state of the art. It is fitted with electric lighting and transparent panels so that visitors can see the inside without entering it.

The cabin is hermetically sealed so that nobody can enter it, not even a mouse. I am sure that in the old days, when Madison lived in it, mice did not have a problem finding their way in through the mud and grass in the cracks of the walls and through the dirt floor.

Halley Park, where the Madison Cabin stood for so long, is a landmark in the Gap. Freighters met there to exchange or sell their goods. Originally there were no trees and no buildings around here. Halley Park was owned by fourteen families.

Situated just outside the original square mile, it became an ice skating rink in 1897. Later the people of Rapid City used it for a picnic place, and it became very popular. Kids spent their summers in Halley Park. In 1934, community gardens were established there. Nowadays, beautiful rosebushes and flowers still thrive in Halley Park.

The original square mile is still the heart of Rapid City, which is now a sprawling, ever-expanding city, reaching out to the north for about three more miles, to the south for six more miles and to the west and east for two or three more miles. The city has long spread beyond the low, but very distinct mountain range of the Hogback so that it now consists of West and East Rapid City.

It would be difficult to commute between the west and east part of town if Rapid Creek had not cut into the sandstone of the Hogback a long time ago and created the Gap. Many businesses—for example, a car repair shop, a dentist's office, an office supply store, a gravestone shop, a little farmers market and a dance studio—are located in the Gap.

Nowadays the Gap is a busy traffic corridor. Not only does a freight train go through, but also two busy streets. The narrow passage naturally causes the abundant stream of traffic to flow quickly, like water that speeds up when it passes through a narrow gorge. The traffic mimics the rapid waters here.

Every day, about 27,000 cars and 800 trucks go through the gap. This is a lot when you consider that we have only a population of about 68,000 people in Rapid City. When I drive through the Gap to get to the other side of town, I enjoy seeing Founders Rock, the rock formation—now so close to the road—that has seen a lot of history. For me, it is the focal point of Rapid City. It all started here when the city founders came in 1876.

Even Founders Rock will not last forever. Wind and weather will slowly destroy the fragile sandstone cliff. Rock climbers like to climb in the middle of the city, even on Founders Rock. They like to use abraded grooves with historic inscriptions in them as hand- and footholds which will also slowly cause the rock to deteriorate.

View from Founders Rock down into the Gap and over to the other side of the Hogback, with Black Hills in the distance

Rapid City turned 140 on February 25 of 2016. So many changes have taken place during these short 140 years since my grandmothers were born. I don't think they would be able to handle the steady stream of traffic through the Gap, the noise of such a big city, the huge population and the fast speed of life. They could probably relate better to the plaque at the base of the Pap Madison cabin that reads:

I was built in the olden golden days,
When this was an unknown land:
My timbers were hewn by a pioneer,
With his rifle near at hand.
I stand as a relic of "Seventy-Six,"
Our nation's centennial year,
That all may see as they enter the hills,
The Home of a pioneer.

(by local historian and teacher R.B. Hughes)

Rapid Creek: From Ripple to Roar

Although it sometimes seems as though Rapid City takes its name from the traffic rushing through it so rapidly, it is really named after Rapid Creek, the mountain stream that rushes through the city, flowing over rocks and forming rapids.

I find it amazing to see such wild flow of water within city limits. Rapid Creek enters town from the southwest, flows through it in a big sweep to the north and then leaves it to the southeast. Right at its entrance into town, Rapid Creek has been dammed, forming Canyon Lake. I love bicycling or walking along the stream and along this lake because the water has such a refreshing, invigorating and cleansing influence.

Rapid Creek flowing through Rapid City

But this river has more to it than just recreational enjoyment. In May and June, when Rapid Creek swells from snowmelt in the mountains and rain, it is a most powerful, roaring river racing through town with a swift, unpredictable current. Every spring, there are warnings not to come too close to the river. It can happen that people are washed away from its banks, get stuck in fallen tree limbs and drown.

In June of 1972, extreme rainfall caused the most detrimental flood in the history of South Dakota. Fifteen inches of rain over six hours made Rapid Creek go over its banks, flooding a wide area and pulling everything with it that was in its way. Not only 1,335 homes, many commercial structures and about 5,000 cars were washed away, but also 238 people lost their lives.

On the southwest side of town, where Rapid Creek enters Canyon Lake, the Jackson Park subdivision was fatally hit. This area had about one hundred residents in forty homes. Only two houses were left standing after the flood, and twenty of the residents drowned in the torrents.

These may be the only two houses left standing after the flood

Not many people know this spot where Rapid Creek enters Canyon Lake. Today we want to see it. We park at the boat launch of the lake. Canyon Lake looks so peaceful with Canada geese, mallards and canvasback swimming on it and a gazebo in the middle. Dammed up like this, Rapid Creek is as gentle as water can be. Only tiny waves ripple the surface. Fishermen sit at the shore, and people bicycle and stroll through the park.

Once this area was three miles out of town, but now it belongs to it. In the old days, there was even a swimming beach at this lake, and I very much regret that it has been removed and replaced by limestone rocks and paved trails. Wouldn't it be fun to come here on hot summer days to swim in the refreshing water? But as you will find later on in this story, we get to swim today anyway, although there is not an official beach anymore.

Canyon Lake

Common merganser

A picnic shelter on the other side of the lake looks rustic and inviting.

Picnic shelter on Canyon Lake

We walk underneath the bridge to the place where Rapid Creek enters Canyon Lake. Once we come out at the other side of the bridge, it feels like being in a remote wilderness, although the traffic of Highway 44 is very close to this spot.

Bridge over Rapid Creek at the entrance to Canyon Lake

These are the grounds where once, before the flood of 1972, the forty houses of the Jackson Park subdivision stood on ten acres. We feel horrified by the thought of twenty people drowning here and thirty-eight homes being swept away in just one night in a torrential flood. What disaster such a normally pleasant river could cause!

The area is now called the Rushmore Lions Nature Park. A few years ago, in 2010, the Rushmore Lions Club volunteered to develop this piece of land into a public park. It cost $12,000 to put the 3/4-mile trail in and to install some benches.

The little park is part of the big flood zone that cuts through Rapid City all the way from the southwest to the southeast. Building is prohibited in this zone. Although brought on by such a catastrophe, this decision to always keep the flood zone free from construction is a very positive development because it allows for a bike path and a green belt all through town.

Trail through Rushmore Lions Nature Park

We walk through the park on the little trail made of crushed rock. Tall grasses, tansies and rampion bellflowers line the path. For a while, the trail follows Rapid Creek, then it leads us over meadows with cottonwood trees.

Showy milkweed along Rapid Creek

Rampion Bellflower

Big, old cottonwood trees have survived the flood of 1972. Imagine, those trees witnessed the flood forty-two years ago and are still standing in the same spot.

Big, old cottonwood trees along our trail

When we look up across the creek, we see hills lined with red limestone. It was a picturesque area to live in—tall trees and the rushing river always close by. Did nobody ever suspect that those houses were built too close to the stream?

View from Rushmore Lions Nature Park up into the surrounding hills

When we pay close attention, we see remnants of the old Jackson Park subdivision and are stunned to find several foundation stones, parts of leftover stone walls and even a doghouse made of natural rock pieces. Near the doghouse, we see a rusty, old water heater with the pipe still attached.

Foundation stone of one of the houses in the Jackson Park Subdivision

Leftover wall, made from fieldstones

Old doghouse, made of natural rock

On a very hot summer day like this, Kent and I like to swim in the waters of the creek. But when we reach the banks today, we see a long, colorful snake curling around some limestone outcroppings. At first I feel hesitant about going into the water, but when Kent identifies the snake as a harmless garter snake, we enter the creek anyway. As usual, we can't stay in for long because this water is so ice-cold that it cools down our inner organs if they are exposed to it for a while.

Swimming in ice-cold Rapid Creek

Strange to think that in the summer of 1971, so many decades ago, the residents of the Jackson Park subdivision probably swam here in the same spot as we do today, not foreboding any catastrophe coming up in June of 1972. Maybe some hardy souls even still swam here in early June of that same year, just days or hours before the disaster struck.

What a beautiful area, and yet, what a tragic memory! This river is unpredictable, like a sleeping lion. As sleek and approachable as a lion at rest may appear, those who know him in his other moods will always be prepared for a sudden change in temperament and a thundering roar.

Deadman Gulch

Last Sunday we met a friendly couple in the woods about five miles from our house. We asked them about other hiking trails around here, and, to our amazement, they told us that there was a trail parallel to the one we were on, and that it was even one mile closer to our home. They said it was called "Deadman Gulch" and seemed to be almost hesitant about recommending a region with such an ugly name.

It might be impossible to walk there, they said, because of the recent storms that had downed so many trees. We would have to park on a driveway leading to a private home. Also, at the end of that trail, we would not have full access to Spring Creek, but would have to cross private property in order to get there.

When looking out of the window this morning, we see a wonder world of hoarfrost. Our willow tree has such a thick layer of frost on it that the branches are being pulled down. All the trees in the neighborhood and even the grass are coated in white. To see more of it, we rush into the woods as soon as possible.

Although we feel shy about parking on private land, we drive up into the dirt road that last Sunday's couple had described. We find a Forest Service gate near a house and squeeze the car into a small spot where we hope not to be in anybody's way. Then we climb over the gate. A very comfortable trail through the frosted pine trees lies before us.

We follow Deadman Creek, which is only partly frozen. In between pine trees and rocks, it bubbles through the grass. There is so much flow of water, and it is green with duckweed, even now during wintertime. This makes us think that this creek never dries out and is fed by springs from the hills around here.

Deadman Gulch trail

Deadman Creek, partly frozen

We have to cross the creek and its tributaries six times, and as there are lots of wet, flooded areas, this is not always easy to do. Because we don't care for balancing over fallen trees to reach the other side, we step from stone to stone and sometimes get a little water in our shoes when the banks are swampy. Sometimes we also cross icy tributaries of Deadman Creek.

Fallen trees over the creek

Kent testing the thickness of the ice on one of the tributaries

After about half an hour on the trail, the sun comes out and the temperature is above freezing. Water starts dripping from the tall pine trees. All of a sudden, it feels like rain is coming down, but it is just thousands of shiny little droplets from the melting hoarfrost.

Shiny droplets on every pine needle

We had no idea about the existence of this gulch and are very surprised by its beauty and grand rock formations. Other people have shown a special interest in this area and put in their mining claims. We see a placer mining claim for a place called "Empty Pockets" and another one for "Six Bit" posted on trees. What do the owners of these claims do? Do they wade through the creek, pan in hand, hoping to find a lump of gold?

The Federal Mining Claim form posted here states that "all persons are warned that disturbance of the monuments, surface, or improvements on this claim or removal of any type without permission of the claimant, will result in their prosecution under the appropriate state and federal statutes." It would be a Class A misdemeanor, punishable by one year in prison or a $100,000 fine.

Does this mean that if I removed a little rock or a piece of wood or even a wildflower from this ground and somebody watched me doing so, I could go to prison for one year? Well, I know for sure that I will not try panning for gold in the duckweed around here.

Federal mining claim of the Six Bit

Just as we are talking about who might have been found dead here in this gulch, giving it such a frightening name, we stumble upon several graves on a slope. Some of them are so overgrown by grass that at first we are not sure whether they are real graves or maybe just some mining holes.

But when we see one of these graves decorated with artificial flowers, we are sure that it is a grave and nothing else. Maybe the grave of a beloved pet? Or have we found *the* dead man's grave, the resting place of the man who lived and died in this canyon a long time ago and, after he was buried here, gave this gulch its grizzly name? Is somebody still taking care of that man's grave and we are standing right in front of it?

Mysterious grave decorated with flowers

The deeper we go into the gulch, the wetter it gets. Again and again, we cross Deadman Creek. Now the canyon walls rise high on both sides. Veins of quartz run through the rocks.

Long veins of quartz in the rocks surrounding the gulch

Tall canyon walls

When we reach a sign stating that this is private property, we know that Spring Creek can't be far anymore. There's no way we would obey the "No Trespassing" sign and turn around now without reaching the stream! We trespass happily into the forbidden ground, and then we see Spring Creek in all its winter beauty.

It's such a feeling of accomplishment to have reached the end of today's trail. Although, as we saw from all these graves and mining claims, Deadman Gulch is obviously known to many people in the area, for us, it is the first time we have set foot into it.

At the outset of today's hike, it was not clear whether we would be able to make it, or whether fallen trees, swampy creek banks and no trespassing warnings would hinder us from reaching Spring Creek. But now we feel almost like Lewis and Clark probing into unknown territory. Or maybe even like the first Native Americans who approached this stream and were delighted to drink from its clear waters.

Spring Creek, partially covered with ice

Little Cabin in the Woods

The first week of September, we go back to basics by living in a rustic hut, eighty-four miles from home. This cabin is in the Black Hills at the Wyoming border, and we rent it from the National Forest Service.

Going there is like falling off the map, because on our regular map of the Black Hills roads this spot is covered by a reference to area maps on the back of it. This means we can't really look for directions to our hut on this map.

Kent goes to a bookstore and finds a special high-resolution map that shows all the details of the cabin's surroundings. Now we know that we have to drive on Highway 16 in the direction of Newcastle and, right after the Wyoming border, turn right onto Boles Canyon Road, which we follow back into South Dakota for twelve miles. Then we will take Road 265 to the left for another three miles to our Summit Ridge cabin.

When we leave for our trip on September 1, we try to follow exactly these directions. We come through lots of construction on Highway 16. As planned, we drive into Wyoming, looking eagerly for that turnoff to Boles Canyon Road.

We pass Road 117, and I shout: "This must have been it, I think we passed it!" Although there was no mention of Boles Canyon Road, I vaguely remember that 117 is its number.

We drive a mile further on Highway 16 until we are able to turn. "Maybe the construction workers took down the 'Boles Canyon Road' sign," Kent assumes. He is right—upon returning to and entering Road 117—we see the sign lying on the ground:

Road sign lying on the ground near the road

We are glad we found the right road. Our vacation starts here. Beautiful limestone ridges stretch out on both sides of Boles Canyon. Only fifteen more miles to our hut!

But we have yet another hindrance to overcome first—some metallic scraping underneath our car. We stop to find out what is going on. We are dragging a blue ribbon behind us. It is attached to a long, long, thin wire of the kind used to bind hay bales together.

This wire is all balled up in a whole cluster which is stuck underneath our car, and we are unable to pull it out. Kent lies down near the car and fumbles and fumbles. I find our kitchen knife in the luggage. Kent snags the wire with it and is finally able to pull it out by one end. We are free to go!

Kent trying to pull the wire from underneath our car

Except for a few big puddles, the gravel roads are in good shape. At the top of the ridge, we reach Summit Ridge cabin at 6,096 feet above sea level. It looks very rustic, made of big, round logs. It was built in 1942 by the Civilian Conservation Corps (CCC).

The roof is covered with two layers of wooden shingles. The outhouse looks as though it was also built of wood, but when we take a closer look, we realize that it is made of cement and then painted.

Summit Ridge Cabin at 6,096 feet

About 150 feet away stands the Summit Ridge Lookout Tower, made of steel and 67.5 feet tall. It was originally built by the CCC on private land, and then in August of 1935 it was skidded cross-country to this permanent location on National Forest land. The move was made by putting the whole steel tower on several big logs and pulling it by two tractors in tandem.

Summit Ridge Lookout Tower

The CCC built and manned many of the twenty-some fire lookout towers in the Black Hills. They are very important for the early detection of fires. About 200 wildfires occur here every year, mainly started by lightning or careless people. We have visited with several fire lookouts on other towers, but the Summit Ridge Tower is not staffed anymore. We are happy about this because we would not like to be watched from above as we cook or laze around our hut.

This tower was manned until 1972. If the fire lookout wanted to cook a meal or needed to go to the restroom, he must have climbed down all the steps to his temporary quarters at the cabin.

Now we finally enter the cabin. A simple padlock secures the door whose combination was given to us by the Hell Canyon District Rangers' Office in an e-mail a few days ago. When we step in, we realize that there is no regular cleaning or maintenance of the hut. Each guest is expected to clean up for the next guest.

The cabin is meant to house up to six people, probably hunters. As I said in the beginning, it is rustic—*really* rustic. The walls are made of round logs, the same logs we have seen from outside. The kitchen has a table with chairs for six, a wood-burning oven, a box for firewood and plywood cabinets. The floor is covered with what must be the original linoleum from 1942.

In the adjacent room are three double-wide bed frames: two stacked as bunk beds and the other hogging the rest of the room. There are no mattresses.

When we open the door to yet another room, we flinch because the first thing we see is a rattrap. Another bunk bed stands in this room, but we never use this room at all and quickly close its door again, not only because of the possible invasion of rats into the main room, but also because of a musty smell in that room. It gives the impression of having once served as a garage.

A layer of grime and dust covers everything in the cabin. The floor and countertops are particularly gross. A little blurry mirror hangs on the wall. Although there is a propane cooking stove and oven, it does not work because it is not connected to any propane. Maybe a propane tank existed when somebody lived here every summer until 1972.

Grimy, dysfunctional propane stove

We see an old-fashioned porcelain sink and a blue hand pump next to it. This water pump looks so ancient that it could well have been installed with the linoleum in 1942. Maybe the CCC even dug a well before they constructed this building. Some plumbing is attached to the pump and sink, but it is loose and useless. Not a drop of water comes from underground. We are truly off the grid. Good thing we brought ten gallons of water with us!

Sink and hand pump in the main room

We have no internet and almost no electricity. When I say "almost" I mean that a little bit of electricity trickles from two small (2.5' x 2') solar panels mounted on the back roof of the cabin. They provide enough power for a lamp in the main room and one in the bedroom—total luxury! But this is as far as modern conveniences go here.

As the sun is setting at 7:20 p.m. this week, it is nice to have some light to eat and read by at night. Kent lights a fire in the iron furnace, and it is very cozy to sit and read. Yes, we are enjoying it, but only until a gnawing noise at the door startles us. "Krrr, krrr, krrr," we hear. This must be the rat trying to join us in the warmth of our cabin. "I found a hole right under the corner of the door, but I plugged it with a little rock," Kent assures me. "So don't worry, he won't get in."

We hang all of our belongings on the few wall hooks and put the rest of it in boxes on top of each other. Nothing is open or on the floor. The gnawing has stopped. We spread our own woolen blanket across the stiff wooden bed board, roll out our self-inflating mattress pads and crawl into our sleeping bags. It is cozy and comfortable. What more does a person need to be happy?

We wake up without rat bites, and our initial misgivings disappear with the rising sun. We enjoy our breakfast in the fresh morning air in front of the cabin. We had originally planned to go away to different places every day. But this first day we enjoy just being here in the silent remoteness so much that we settle in and feel at home. By Day 5, we live here. All the inherited grime and dirt has become ours.

We would not leave at all, but after five days, we have to return to civilization to recharge our battery-operated devices and check our e-mail. If we weren't so backward and had a smartphone, we could have been checking e-mail all the time because the reception on the summit is great. But even without the benefit of modern communications, we can hear a hot bath calling. It's time to head home.

Our little cabin in the woods

Unusual Dwellings in the Black Hills

On just one hike from Reeder Ranch off Sheridan Lake Road down to the Methodist Camp, we see several most uncommon dwelling places. The wooden structure pictured below we spot near a pond in the woods. From afar, it looks like a birdhouse perched on a very tall pole. What kind of bird would want to live in such a dwelling place? It's too big for bluebirds and does not have the right shape for an osprey or owl. But actually, it is not for birds at all! We find that out when we go closer and read a sign at the foot of the pole:

POSTED: FOREST SERVICE BAT NURSERIES Eagle Project by Joel Bice DO NOT DISTURB

Bat nursery on top of a pole

This wooden box above our heads is a maternity roost box. There are probably three to four hundred female bats hanging upside down from the ceiling. During the night, they are active and feeding. Every night, an adult bat catches thousands of insects. In a few weeks in June, they will give birth to pups, which they will nurse with their milk. The baby bats will be clinging to their mothers' nipples and sucking. The males roost on their own or in small groups somewhere else in hollow trees, caves or unused buildings.

Bat nursery from below

This is not the only strange dwelling place we encounter today. When we follow the trail down to Spring Creek, we see two old, weathered outhouses in the woods. They don't really seem to belong here.

In faded letters, we read the name "Herman" on one of them. Who is Herman? We don't want to disturb him, but I am so curious to find out more that I slowly open the door. This is what we see inside:

Herman's box in the old outhouse

There is still the question: Who is Herman? A raccoon, a squirrel, a porcupine or skunk? I don't think a porcupine or skunk would be able to jump up into the entrance hole. Herman's box is about twenty inches tall, and it looks comfortable and roomy, but he does not seem to be at home. Maybe he heard us coming and escaped through the quite big hole at the bottom of the outhouse side wall.

When I later ask the Forest Service about Herman's box, they say it is a typical owl house. But now that it is inside the outhouse with the entrance hole down at the bottom, it looks as though a squirrel or packrat has taken over and is using it for its own nesting purposes.

Old outhouse in the woods

We look into the other outhouse and find an empty nest in one corner. Or is it only nesting material, loosely deposited here? Whatever animal lives here, it must be a bird because the entrance consists of a small hole above the door. But when I later ask the Forest Service about this nest, they tell me it looks like that of a chipmunk or packrat because those animals loosely throw sticks, grass and leaves in a pile to live in.

Disorderly nest in the other outhouse

When we cross Spring Creek, we see the cabins of the Methodist Camp nestled in the woods. What a rustic, but comfortable place to live for a few weeks during the summer! The youngsters live in these cabins and eat, pray, play, fish, swim, sing and hike together. In the evenings, when sitting at the campfire and listening to ghost stories, they sense the bats flying overhead. Maybe some of these bats live in the abandoned gold mine on campus.

At night, when lying in their bunk beds, they hear thunder over the mountains, owls hooting overhead, coyotes yipping in the woods and the creek rushing over rocks and rapids nearby. I bet, for some of these children, these are odd noises that scare them in the beginning, but at least they have the wooden cabin walls around them and a roof that keeps the rain out.

After being startled by unusual night sounds like squealing and howling the first few nights, the children will get used to life in a cabin and sleep soundly through the night. When they return home, they will have extraordinary stories to tell about bat nurseries, Herman the Unknown, a Packrat's nest in an outhouse and sleeping in their cabin in the woods.

Cabin of the Methodist church camp at Spring Creek

Lost in the Wild

From time to time, we see newspaper reports about tourists or even people from around here who get lost in the Black Hills. We often wonder how it is possible to get lost in an area that has so much housing and so many roads cutting through. Do those people have no sense of direction? Can't they orient themselves by looking at the position of the sun? That's what we keep thinking, but last weekend we were knocked off our perch, and from now on, we won't wonder anymore when somebody loses his orientation in the hills.

It happens like this: We want to hike on Trail #40, the Deerfield Trail from Kinney Canyon to Deerfield Lake. In the beginning, it goes well—we find the trail and happily walk along until we come to a sign that indicates we should leave the wider trail and walk upwards. We obey and walk through a landscape like this:

Do you see the small trail?

The trail is small, but well defined, and everything is still fine, until that little trail peters out and we stand in front of a hindrance. Many fallen trees lie crosswise in our way. At this point, we should recognize that we are on the wrong track and should return to the bigger trail.

Fallen trees lying crisscross in our way

But we have already walked for half an hour down this path and are loathe to turn around. We think we are still in the right direction and the lake should be visible soon. So we continue, trying to orient ourselves by the position of the sun. But that is more difficult than we think. How far have we already gone? Shall we proceed toward the south or west? We continue climbing over these fallen trees, then over some more fallen trees and through the thickness of the forest.

Two gray jays are flying in front of us, as though they want to show us the way. From time to time, they perch on a tree and look at us. I guess they don't see many people coming through this neck of the woods.

Gray jay on a tree in the wilderness

As we have not seen any more trail signs since we left the big trail, we start wondering where we are and where we are going. Uprooted tree stumps and large stands of thistles do not make our walking any easier.

"Wouldn't it make sense to return to the big trail?" I ask, but we have no idea anymore how to retrace our steps. "Let's go further down." Kent replies, "I see the tops of a few spruce growing over there." The dryness of the southern hills favors ponderosa pine, so the presence of spruce is often a sign of a small creek. We think that rivulet might flow toward the lake.

So we bushwhack our way further down and indeed come to a clear stream, bubbling steadily over the rocks. As it is no fun to get wet feet in October, we stay a little higher above the creek and finally find a place where we are able to cross it. "Wouldn't it be great to see the Trail #40 sign again?" Kent asks. "Yes, this would be like being in the desert and coming upon a sign that announces an oasis within a few hundred feet," I agree. Kent crosses the creek first and shouts: "I see a trail!" And indeed there it is on the other slope, very easy to walk and leading us toward the lake! Within a few steps, we even find the Trail #40 sign. Now it does not take us long to reach Castle Creek.

Castle Creek near Deerfield Lake

A little further, we reach the spillway and then the dam of Deerfield Lake. Castle Creek is gushing out of an opening underneath a building at the foot of the dam like water would gush out of a bathtub drain. We can hear the sputtering water all the way to where we stand.

Castle Creek rushing out of Deerfield Lake below the dam

Now Trail #40 leads us up to the high plain above the lake. At this time of year, the grass is brownish-gray. We love to look into the vastness of the plateau like this.

High plains above Deerfield Lake

But where is the lake? Finally we catch a glimpse of it, and then we stand at its northern shore.

Glimpse of the northern part of Deerfield Lake

Standing at the shore of Deerfield Lake

Wilted wildflowers at the northern part of Deerfield Lake

Having looked at the clear waters of this quiet lake, we could now just turn around and go back to the car on the correct path. But—I am not sure how it happens—when we come to the point where we took the wrong trail on our way to the lake, this time, we decide *not* to go back the way we came, but to take a "shortcut" that we expect to be the true and easy trail.

At least the trail we take now looks better than the other one that went cross-country. We think it will lead us directly to the car. It is a nice, wide trail, and we trust it. "If it does not take us in the right direction, we can always retrace it back to this starting point," we think.

Although this trail keeps wrapping a little further south than we expected, it is such a good, comfortable walk that we are convinced its meandering will eventually take us into the right direction and we will soon find the car.

So we wander along leisurely, until the trail gets smaller and smaller and finally peters out. What is it about this region that even the most promising trails simply dissolve into the wilderness? Do we retrace our steps to the point where we took the wrong path? No, of course not. We seem to love adventure.

But after about one-and-a-half hours, we are not so sure anymore. Again, the sun does not help us much. We know that the sun is more to the west now, but in which direction is our car? Directly east, or more to the north now? Have we walked in circles?

We walk through tall grass with rocks and tree stumps underneath and squeeze ourselves under and between fallen trees. We are suppressing any thought that rattlesnakes might be hiding exactly in such places where we put our feet.

It is getting worse and worse. Now we are in the middle of a field of thick thistles that sting through our pants. Many times we have to go around thickets of dead trees, intermingled with all kinds of brambles that are too dense to penetrate. The terrain we are walking across looks like this:

Wilderness somewhere near Deerfield Trail

Again, we have this uneasy feeling that we could be going in circles. But now we no longer have unlimited time to find our car. In two hours, the sun will be down. Night is when the Black Hills are worthy of their name. It is new moon and it would be too dangerous to step even one foot in the difficult terrain. We know for sure that we have to be back to the car by sunset.

It gives us some hope when we catch a glimpse of a ranch house on a faraway hill. But how would we get there? Would those people even be home? And we really want to be back at the car, not knocking at the door of that ranch house when the sun is down.

So we try to steadily go down into the valley because we parked in a valley. But is this our valley? You see, how even our thinking gets a little confused by all of this erring around in the wilderness? Kent starts mentally planning beds of pine needles and moss that might keep us warm during the cold October night. "We have to gather all this material before the sun is down," he asserts. But I have no inclination to shiver out here in an earth hole in the wilderness, covered with pine needles. We push on toward the valley.

When we reach a fence, we feel happy because it is a sign of civilization. We crawl through, walk over a cow pasture and finally see a corral and a dirt road. We manage to work our way around all the fences that enclose the corral and around a stock pond, and then we are on the road!

As I remember coming by a corral on our way to the trailhead, we know which direction we have to walk on the road in order to find our car. The corral is indeed quite a ways south of where we had expected that enticing trail to take us. We were not hopelessly lost, but if we had not emerged from the bramble around now, there's a good possibility we would have been listening to the hooting of owls all night.

We made it and will be more careful next time we hike. Shall we admit that we took no flashlights, no compass, no GPS, that there was no cell phone service out there, and that Kent even left his hat and coat behind? He is usually so careful about heeding the Boy Scout motto: "Be prepared."

What were we thinking of when we ambled complacently down a trail we had never tried before? The day had been so warm and promising and the trail so well-defined when we left the car that we had considered it only a Sunday stroll through the woods. Kent says he should turn in his old Scouting merit badges.

Also, now that we have managed to get lost twice in one day, we will never again make fun of anybody who gets lost in the wilderness of the Black Hills.

Hot Hike to Black Elk Peak

At our age, it is good to choose special hiking highlights each birthday in order to confirm for ourselves that we are still in good enough shape to reach these highlights. Last year, we hiked to the top of Little Devils Tower. I am happy to say that hike seemed easier than when we last did it ten years ago.

This year I choose the summit of Black Elk Peak (formerly Harney Peak), the highest peak east of the Rockies, as the destination for eating my rhubarb birthday pie. Will we still be able to make it? Officially, it takes only three to four hours for the seven miles leading up to and coming down from the summit. I remember that, last time, it took us five hours.

Our goal: Black Elk Peak

As the morning is cloudy, gray and cool in Rapid City, we are not in a hurry to leave for our hike. I take birthday phone calls from Germany and open birthday cards and gifts.

When we arrive at the trailhead, it is already noontime. We soon discover that starting so late was a mistake because the sun is coming out, and it is getting hotter and hotter.

Also: The landscape has changed since we last hiked here. Many trees have been taken out because of the pine beetle infestation. Many of the remaining trees are also brown or black and standing there like skeletons. Some places are covered with fallen, dead trees. This means we are not walking in the shade of trees most of the time anymore, but in the full sunshine, which makes our hike much more cumbersome than expected.

Nevertheless, some of the views are even better than before. Early on, we can see Little Devils Tower and then the fire tower on top of Black Elk Peak in the distance.

Many dead and fallen trees on our way to Black Elk Peak

Little Devils Tower

First glimpse of the Black Elk Peak tower on our hike

When we reach the only creek of this hike, we sit down in the shade of some trees and have lunch.

Lunch place at the creek

Now the trail becomes more strenuous because it gets steeper and is strewn with boulders of all sizes.

Rocky trail to the summit

After scrambling along in the heat for a while, we get rewarded by closer views of the tower. We also have stunning views of Little Devils Tower and, from a little higher up, the Cathedral Spires and the mountain chains behind them.

Cathedral Spires

Almost on the top, we go over a staircase and finally into the tower. There is nothing more elating than standing on top of a mountain in the fresh summer breeze after a long, hot hike and enjoying the view. Everywhere we look, there is the greenness of June. Only a small mountain to the north, Storm Hill, sits charred, recovering from a recent fire. Otherwise, the overall impression is the utter beauty of the Black Hills in early summer.

From here, we have a 360^0 view over the Black Hills and even into Rapid City, Hill City and Custer. We realize that we now recognize much more of our surroundings than last time we were here. We can now name many of the mountains, for example Storm Mountain, Boulder Hill, Silver Mountain, because we have been there. This is what Little Devils Tower looks like from here:

Cathedral Spires to the left, Little Devils Tower in the center

We don't even have to look so far out to see spectacular sites, but when we look at the rocks closer to the tower, a mountain goat comes into view. For a while, it stands motionless on top of a rocky precipice before it jumps over to another rock and disappears. Except for its legs, it looks shorn. Who was able to catch the mountain goat to shear it?

Mountain goat on the rocks

Below the tower we see an old, bent-over spruce with lots of prayer cloths tied to it. Native Americans must feel that this is an auspicious site to offer prayer ties to the Great Spirit.

Spruce with prayer cloths on it

After sitting in the shade of the spruce for a while and eating the rhubarb birthday pie, we feel that it is time to start the descent. "We are the only ones left near the tower and will be the last ones to come down from the mountain," we think. But far from it! After descending the staircases from the tower, we see an elderly couple making their way up. "Well, these are the longest days of the year, and if they don't dawdle too long on the summit, they will still make it down by daylight," we say to each other in a reassuring way, and we assume that these two must have really been the last latecomers.

We hike slowly over the boulder path for about half an hour, when we hear voices coming from below. It is 7 p.m. and we had not expected any more stragglers. It amazes us even more when we see that the couple still making their way up is also elderly and huffing and puffing. "You dare to climb up at this time of the day," we say to them. "Are you sure you will make it all the way down during daylight?"

Well, they think they will make it. Their friends, the couple we saw earlier, left them behind, and now they are struggling to catch up with them. These must, for sure, have been the last ones coming up today! We think they miscalculated the length of the trail and will have to find their way down in the moonlight. Luckily, it is just about full moon, so they will be safe.

To our amazement, shortly afterwards, we encounter yet another group of people. They are sitting and lying on the rocks near the trail, looking like they are in some kind of trance, contemplating something or worshipping nature. They have backpacks with them and seem to be equipped for a night in the woods. "Are you camping out here?" Kent asks one of them. "Just resting," is the short answer. We feel that they are absorbed in some otherworldly state and don't bother them any further. At least they won't attempt to hike to the summit anymore today!

You would not believe it, but around 7:45 p.m., we pass yet another group of people coming up the trail. They are a Native American family, each of them carrying nothing but one water bottle. "Are you still going to make it all the way up?" we ask in disbelief. "Yes, we will," is their answer.

Now this must be some kind of vision quest or some ritual they follow. Maybe their plan is to go up in the last light of the day and then come down in the moonlight. It does not seem that they carry any warmer clothing or flashlights for the night. We hope they will make it okay. They speak with such assurance that we feel they will be safe.

When we reach our car we are happy that we did it, and that we had such a perfect birthday walk. But it would not hurt to start out earlier in the morning or to choose a cooler day for our next big hike.

Sign of Love Above Custer

Many US cities feature signs with their name or the name of one of their dominant attractions on a mountaintop above the city. For example, when reaching Hollywood, you can read its name from far away in gigantic, white letters mounted on posts. It is surrounded by a tall fence, and cameras surveil it day and night. Nevertheless, there are some people who cannot be stopped by a fence or cameras and are determined to reach their dreams and touch the Hollywood Sign.

In South Dakota, we also have towns with big signs on a nearby mountaintop. For example, above the town of Sturgis is a big sign on a mountain that reads "STURGIS."

Above Rapid City, we have a sign reading "**SMD**," which stands for South Dakota School of Mines, our engineering college. It is made of white cement, and in the homecoming ceremony, students whitewash it every year in September. The students pour white paint solution over the sign and then slide down on it, a quite messy affair.

CUSTER sign on a mountain above Custer

The town of Custer also has a sign, reading "CUSTER." When driving through Custer, we have seen it many times on a mountain above town. Electric light bulbs inside this sign make it glow at night. We have often thought that it would be nice to stand by the sign and see Custer and the surrounding mountains from above.

We are not sure whether there is a trail up to the sign, but today we'll try to get to it. In downtown Custer we find stairs that lead us higher and higher up the mountain. We arrive at a lookout point and have a good view of Custer and Buckhorn Mountain behind it.

City of Custer and Buckhorn Mountain from above

But we have not yet reached the CUSTER sign. "Where is it?" we ask each other. Two people who grew up in Custer happen to be standing on the lookout with us. They overhear us and point over to the other side of the mountain ridge: "It's over there," they explain. "There's no real trail to it, but we can take you there." What serendipity that they are right here to lead us when we need them! Here you see them guiding us over boulders in the direction of the sign.

Do you see the big letters of the sign coming up on top of the rock?

When we reach the sign, we try to take photos of it, but it stands directly on the brink of a cliff, and we can't step further out in front of it without falling into the abyss. So we can only get part of the sign on our photo:

We are right there at the sign!

Our guides tell us that the sign once displayed a different word—"LOVE"—for just one evening. It was in the '70s, at the prom of our tour guides' brother. He and some others in his senior class had the idea to play a special graduation prank. Before the prom, they worked out a plan, went up to the CUSTER sign and monkeyed with it. They unscrewed the light bulbs in the letters C and R, turned off parts of others and strung some lighting to make new parts. I don't know how exactly they did it, but the result was astounding, and a whole new word emerged.

Sometime during the dance, somebody happened to look up to the sign and shouted: "Hey, look up at the Custer sign! What's going on? The sign reads 'LOVE'!"

I guess the town fathers were not very happy about this event and had the sign go dark within half an hour, but I think it showed quite some ingenuity, spirit and boldness. Probably I like this prank so much because I used to be a rebel in the 1970s myself.

What these young people did required so much more resourcefulness than just spraying the graffiti that covers the letters today. Those young people had the electrical know-how to make things happen. They did not harm anybody or anything. After the prom, somebody did of course have to fumble with the sign to get the light bulbs to display the intended name again. But it had all been clean fun.

The authorities never found out who was responsible for this prank. How strange it is that, for the short time it lasted, LOVE was threatening to the local peace officers that night. Why did it have to be extinguished so quickly? I find the graffiti sprayed all over the sign today much more disturbing.

Here's a thought: Just as Rapid City students whitewash their mountain sign each year, wouldn't it be a pleasant gesture in Custer to let local students remove the graffiti from their own town sign before each prom and, for just one evening a year, let LOVE return to the mountain?

Standing in front of the CUSTER sign
that is now sprayed with graffiti

Spokane—Mining Town from 1890

When you hear about the 1874 Gold Rush in the Black Hills and of the men who came from far and wide to try their luck and often risk their health and lives to make a fortune, it sounds like a story from long ago. Old names like Deadman Gulch, Iron Mountain, Silver City, Big Thunder Gold Mine, Holy Terror Gold Mine or Wade's Gold Mill remind us of those adventurous times. But, other than these names, are there any palpable traces of the exploration for gold, silver and other minerals still to be found today?

We often find conical holes in the ground, indicating that people have dug for gold in those places. Many of the miners lived simply in tents, and any traces of those dwellings are long gone. Some of them, especially after they found some gold, built cabins and houses for themselves and even got their wives or families to join them.

What became of all those structures? From time to time, we see a shed or house where miners lived, still standing. But we have also heard that there were many little towns all over the Black Hills that once boomed and then disappeared as fast as they sprung up.

One of these towns, Spokane, is still there, even though it is now bedraggled and close to ruin. We have heard about this town for years, an original mining site from 1890. It formed around a mine, supplying zinc, lead, silver, hematite, graphite, beryl, mica, copper and gold. We have no idea where it is located and are amazed to read in our newspaper that it is not far from a road we have driven dozens of times to get to our favorite lake.

Upon arrival, we are even more amazed at how easy it is to reach Spokane. Just a short walk on an old overgrown dirt road, and we see some dilapidated buildings, leaning in all directions. They stand on a wide meadow, and higher up on a slope we see more buildings hidden in the woods.

Now you might think: "What's so special about some rickety old buildings, ready to collapse?" Let me show you a few of those buildings and some of the other things that explain how people lived here, where they got their water, how they went to get their supplies from the bigger cities and how they stored their food. Even a grave can be found higher up near the mining site.

One of the buildings is a wooden structure covered with corroded sheet metal. Through the window holes, we can look right through the building. Maybe this was just a shed, or was it a miner's cabin? Grasses, thistles and ferns grow inside the cabin on the dirt floor, and the wind whistles through the building.

Building covered with sheet metal

Thistles and ferns inside the cabin

Not far from it is an equally dilapidated wooden outhouse. All the buildings stand in tall grass, and wildflowers grow around them.

Outhouse in Spokane

Some bigger houses, also in desolate condition, stand on the same meadow. We are lucky to see them this summer because they might not make it through another winter. We don't dare enter this house:

Ready to fall to the ground

In the middle of an aspen grove, we discover this stately building that also has seen better times.

Rather big building in an aspen grove

Seeing so many buildings here poses several questions. For example: Did the miners go the 6.6 miles to Keystone to get their supplies? Or was Rockerville, about ten miles away, a better option for them in those days? Or were they quite self-sufficient? I assume that around 1890 they did not often travel to Rapid City as this would have been a journey of 23 miles and would have taken quite a long time to ride there through the woods. In the early days, they must have taken horses or horse-drawn carts to go to a bigger city.

Later on, they had cars and trucks, and up to this day the battered, rusty remains of those vehicles still stand here in the woods. They are in extremely bad condition. The wheels and upholstery are gone, rusty box springs can be seen where seats once were. Grass grows through the floors. As we are no car experts, we cannot tell the make or age of the wrecks, but we estimate that they are from as early as the 1940s, from the time when cars became popular in the US and when Spokane was abandoned.

Some of them seem to be from the 1950s. We don't like the fact that the people of Spokane left their old cars like this, deteriorating in the woods for ages to come. This car looks like a Ford from the 1950s:

Battered old cars in the woods

Not only cars were abandoned when the miners left Spokane. We also see old tin cans in a pit, rusting away through the ages. I bet even Sherlock Holmes would not be able to figure out who ate from these cans and when, and what they contained.

Rusty old tin bucket hanging from a tree

We see a rusty old tin bucket hanging from a tree. Did it once contain gold or silver? Or was it maybe used to fetch water from Spokane Creek, one thousand feet away?

We wonder whether Spokane Creek was their only source of water. If yes, wouldn't it have been more practical to settle closer to the creek? But their main focus was with the mine, and they wanted to be very close to it; water was only a subordinate requirement.

In later years, they excavated a cistern which we discover on the woody slope. The cistern is very deep and made of cement. The heavy lid is half open and hard to move. It would be very dangerous if a child or a dog fell in here!

Deep cistern

Close to the cistern is another structure made of cement. It looks like a sturdy bunker, built into the slope. We enter it and see empty wooden shelves along the wall. This must have been a root cellar.

Sturdy root cellar

It does not look big enough to have served the whole town. But for one household alone, it looks too big. This brings up the question of how communal life was structured in the early days. It was not until 1927 that a schoolhouse was built. Also, we have not heard about or seen a church building. It seems that the community had its emphasis on the mine. Every man worked at the mine and they all depended on it. Was this a company town, where everything was owned by the mine?

On what terms did all these people live with each other here in 1890 and later? Did they help each other survive the harsh winters, or were they in competition? Many of them might have been kind and helpful to their neighbors, but not all of them were in good standing with each other. Sometimes greed for gold could even end in murder.

On a high meadow, surrounded by pine trees, we come by a place marked with rocks and a headstone. It looks fresh and new, as if it was put there only recently. A tiny American flag is sticking in the ground, a few special rocks, such as quartz, are put around the stone, and some coins are lying on it.

The letters engraved on the headstone read:

IN LOVING MEMORY FROM HIS GRANDCHILDREN
JAMES FERNANDO SHEPHERD
FEB. 3, 1850 TO JUNE 21, 1908
MURDERED OVER A MINING CLAIM

Headstone of the miner's grave

What happened here? The grandchildren of the murdered man probably put up the headstone long after the murder. Most likely they did not know their grandfather in person, but heard of the story and wanted to give him a proper memorial. We wonder how the custom of putting coins on the gravestone emerged.

Murdered miner's grave

Very close to the grave stands the house of the mine's manager on top of the hill. It has two stories and would look quite inviting, if it wasn't so run down.

Manager's home

How surprised we are when we see old-fashioned knob-and-tube electric lines running into the house. There is even an old gas stove in the kitchen. We hear that the house was not abandoned until the 1970s.

Stove in the manager's house

Lots of pine cones have been blown in through the window openings. The wall paper is flaking off in big chunks. Doors, windows and parts of the inner and outer walls are missing altogether.

Pine cones blown in through the window holes

We don't think this house could be fixed up again, but it stands at such a pretty location in the middle of the pine forest that we almost envy the prior owners. But did they still have to go down to the cistern to fetch their water in buckets? Where is the outhouse? Considering all of this, we think we are better off in our home in Rapid City.

On the slope near the manager's home, we see dozens of mining holes, round pits in the ground, about five feet deep. There is no knowing whether the miners found any minerals so close to the surface.

The main mine shaft went further into the ground. It is blocked from the public by a fence. Heavy iron posts enclose the actual site of the mine shaft in a rectangle. Maybe they once held another fence. It might be dangerous to walk over this parcel of land because the shaft underneath still exists and could collapse.

At least one building, maybe the entrance to the shaft, stood within the rectangle, as we can see from its footprint on the grass. But it has been removed by the Forest Service.

Site of the former mine shaft

From seeing all of this, we don't get the impression that Spokane was a very successful town. But it actually had very good times. In 1927, just two years before the USA went into the Great Depression, Spokane had one of its best years. The town's profits totaled $144,742. A school was built, and new miners came to town. But soon the mine began to fail and had to be closed in 1940. This was the time when the miners began to leave, and the town became abandoned.

There was one last attempt in 1950 to reopen the mine, but it failed. Buildings burned down, and the US Forest Service destroyed some of them because they were not safe.

Until the mid-1980s, a watchman was on guard over the old town. Can you imagine walking through a ghost town night after night, all by yourself? Did the watchman live in one of those buildings?

I wonder if he was armed and whether he ran into problems from time to time, such as homeless people sleeping in the ruins or youngsters coming with graffiti cans to adorn the old walls. Finally maintaining the watch was not feasible anymore, and the town was officially abandoned.

Today we got an impression of Spokane and how it developed, but to really know what was going on here and how it felt to live among the miners, we would have to dig deeper into history. We would need to find old court documents or old letters from this time or maybe some account of the stories that James Fernando Shepard, his children or his murderer or others from this region harbored.

Do such accounts exist? After all, more than a century is a long time, and it might be easier to find gold than to discover what day-to-day reality was like in the early days here in Spokane.

Railroad Bed in a Most Remote Canyon

Looking down at Knife Blade Rock in Big Elk Canyon, I can't imagine a more remote and inaccessible landscape. Knife Blade Rock looks just like the big blade of an old-fashioned knife. Spruce and pine trees grow along the rock and even on the very top of it. Big Elk Creek winds around this remarkable rock that stands all alone, pointing heavenwards in a basin formed by limestone cliffs.

Looking down to Knife Blade Rock in Big Elk Canyon

Has anybody ever been down in this canyon or on top of Knife Blade Rock? The cliffs are so steep that we can't even hope to reach their bottom. But then we find a trail a few miles further northwest that takes us right down into the canyon on an easy slope, and we can cross Big Elk Creek.

Crossing Big Elk Creek

Today we won't make it all the way down to Knife Blade Rock, but we discover something interesting on our trail—piles of rocks raised like a railroad bed. "What's this?" I ask Kent. "It looks like a dam or some other kind of man-made construction." "Well, yes, it seems to be an old railroad bed," Kent replies. Although covered with grass, moss and trees, it sure has the shape of an embankment and is running very straight. I have a hard time believing that a railroad once chugged through this quiet, remote canyon. But Kent assures me that in the gold rush era many railroads connected the different camps and towns in the Black Hills, and now there is barely any trace of them left in most cases.

Back home I try to find out more online about this mysterious railroad. Part of the Black Hills & Ft. Pierre Railroad, it really existed from 1890 to 1907 in Big Elk Canyon. In those seventeen years, it connected Piedmont with Lead, running once a day. Its stations—Bucks, Anthonys, Holloway, Mowatt, Runkles (there is still a Runkle Road), Crystal Cave (now Bethlehem Cave), Jones, Doyles, Calcite and Gardners—most of them probably mining sites, are not on the map anymore.

It was the first railroad in the Black Hills. Can you imagine what this means—finally having a railroad in this area? It was a world-shaking event as it meant a different, new means of transportation than just traveling by foot, horse, stagecoach, oxen and mule teams. A whole new era was about to begin.

Railroad through Big Elk Canyon in 1890
[From an article "Black Hills and Fort Pierre Railroad" found on Wikipedia on May 6, 2015]

Today it takes thirty-nine minutes to drive the thirty-one miles of Interstate and highway from Piedmont to Lead. But this railroad went more directly, through Big Elk Canyon—an engineering masterpiece, you might say. Or a very foolish undertaking, as we will soon see.

The straight-line distance between the two towns is twenty miles, but I don't know how many miles of rail were laid so that this railroad could make its way through the rocks, always close to the river, with many tight hairpin curves and steep grades.

Originally this line hauled lumber, supplies and machinery to the gold mine operations of the Homestake Company in Lead. You can see timber and some other load on the last three wagons of the above photo. Several passengers seem to have ridden the train in the windowless cattle car behind the locomotive on the day the photo was taken. We see them standing by the train. When riding a train through such a spectacular canyon, I would have wanted to look out the windows to take the whole scenery in. On other photos, I notice that there were also trains with passenger coaches that had windows.

This railroad even curved around Knife Blade Rock, as we can see on old postcards. So, if we had stood at our panoramic outlook over one hundred years ago, we would not have looked down a serene and undisturbed chasm, but might have seen a steam locomotive huffing and puffing up the canyon and circling around Knife Blade Rock.

I am not sure what the reason for this horseshoe curve was. I don't think the engineers would have done the extra construction of more railroad ties just for fun and sightseeing purposes. Were they not afraid of flash floods from Big Elk Creek, just a few feet away? How could they possibly have contained Big Elk Creek and protected the railroad from it when it was bursting its banks in a strong rain or snowmelt?

And yes, there was a big flood. On June 13, 1907, it came roaring down Big Elk Canyon and destroyed nine miles (other sources report fifteen miles) of track and many bridges. Railroad ties were washed downstream as far as fifty miles. This was the end of this very line through Big Elk Canyon, but the Black Hills & Ft. Pierre Railroad continued for twenty-three more years on an alternate route, still connecting Piedmont and Lead.

Knife Blade Rock recovered from all the railroad hustle and bustle around it, and nature regained its natural state. When we look down there now, we can't imagine that there once was a major industrial enterprise chugging in and out of the folds of these mountains.

Horseshoe Curve around Knife Blade Rock in 1908

In the 1920s, automobile traffic increased, mining activities decreased and the railroad from Piedmont to Lead was not needed much anymore. It finally closed in 1930 and was dismantled.

But besides the weathered piles of rock testifying to its existence in Big Elk Canyon, there is still one big building from 1901 that was essential for the functioning of this railroad—the roundhouse in Lead. It included a railway turntable, a device for turning locomotives so that they could be moved back in the direction from which they came. Fifteen to twenty skilled men once serviced and repaired engines and railroad equipment in this building. They worked twelve-hour shifts seven days a week.

Strong winters with heavy snow and ice made railroading dangerous. Many railroad men lost their lives in this region, and many wrecks occurred. The equipment was repaired in the roundhouse, and soon the trains were back on the tracks. As the railroad played such a vital role in the mining business, the Homestake Mine was very quick and determined to repair it whenever needed.

After 1930 the roundhouse served as a truck garage, retail outlet and storage facility. It fell into disrepair and was supposed to be torn down. But then a business man bought it in order to save the last railroad structure in Lead from destruction. It was restored and now is a fine restaurant. In this way, a historic building that once served as the key hub of railroad activity could be saved.

Roundhouse of the Black Hills & Ft. Pierre Railroad in Lead

Just over a century ago, a seething mass of miners populated every gulch, and a net of railroads covered the Black Hills. In our time, masses of tourists swarm the Hills every summer in countless cars, ATVs and motorcycles.

How will the situation change in another one hundred years? I hope there will be zero-emission vehicles, driving by themselves. Or will the roads disappear altogether as we hover above the treetops in drones, allowing the forest to return to its remote, seemingly untouched state for unspoiled hikes?

Scenic—Changes of Scene over Time

On our way to the Badlands, we come by Scenic, a tiny ghost town of only about ten inhabitants. Situated 45 miles southeast of Rapid City, it is one of those towns in South Dakota that have seen better times.

With ghost towns in the Black Hills, it is obvious why they sprang up in the late 1880s. It was the gold rush that drew people into those hilly regions. But why would anybody even have the idea to found a town in the semi-arid prairie region next to the Badlands where Scenic Township is now located? There is no water, no gold, no oil and no fertile soil.

The closest river is the Cheyenne, seven miles away. In the old days, the Cheyenne River was the primary source of running water for Scenic. We wonder whether they really had to ride seven miles on horseback for every drop of water needed. How did they do their laundry, how did they ever take a bath? With an annual precipitation of sixteen inches, water must have been a scarcity.

I can think of only one reason for Scenic to emerge: it sits where, in the 1880s, the Chicago, Milwaukee, St. Paul and Pacific Railroad passed near the fork of a long road that goes south into the Pine Ridge reservation and another road that goes eastward from Rapid City. People settled here and eventually established the town of Scenic in 1906.

These two roads are still used a lot today. Travelers from the central part of the Pine Ridge reservation come by here daily on their way to Rapid City. Tourists and motorcyclists visiting the Badlands stop by, too. As small, lifeless and decrepit as it looks nowadays in the winter, it must have once been a bustling little community, and, now that the gas station has reopened, it still attracts people to stop here, look around, get gas and maybe even stay a little longer to shop and eat and drink.

When we first drive into Scenic we wonder about the name because it does not look scenic at all. It is flat and rather boring. I can't say that there are especially good views right here in town. But then I hear that the town fathers named it for the great views of the Badlands. When driving a few miles further, we know what they meant—Scenic is the gateway to the Badlands, and the views of the scraggy moonscapes are fantastic.

Sheep Mountain Table south of Scenic

The heyday of Scenic was in 1915 when it enjoyed its largest population of 155 residents. At its peak, this typical Old West town had two restaurants, a saloon, three gas stations, a hotel, train depot, dance hall, school, bank, jail, post office, bunkhouse, museum and two stores. We are amazed at how many different businesses and governmental buildings a small town of 155 inhabitants needed and how they were able to provide all of this.

But why they needed three gas stations remains a mystery to us. Ranchers rode to town from the surrounding homesteads or they came by horse-drawn wagon to drink, dance, eat, shop, mail letters, do their banking, and so on. The ranchers' children had to walk to the Scenic school, often from many miles away.

Seeing the town now, we can't imagine how lively it was just a few decades ago. An elderly woman once told us that she had gone to the Scenic dance hall for a prom in the 1950s. It was in May, the weather was warm, and everybody was dressed in their light prom dresses.

But as so often happens in South Dakota, the weather changed that night, and a blizzard came up. At first the dancers did not notice what was going on, but when they wanted to return home late that night, they realized that the snow had enclosed them and they could not escape the dance hall. Wearing only prom dresses and fine suits, they were trapped by the blizzard. I don't remember now how long it took them to finally get home and whether they got a cold from this adventure, but at least they were all alive and able to relate this story decades later to newcomers like us.

We are not sure which one of the forty or so remaining buildings was the dance hall. Most of them are made of wood and more or less decrepit and falling apart. The town stretches over twelve acres and consists of about one hundred small lots.

Some of the buildings are padlocked and have plywood over their windows and doors, but the spirit of the old time is still present: About three dozen old cattle skulls are hanging above the sign over the Longhorn Saloon. The sign announces that the saloon was constructed in 1906. It also indicates what you can get and do here—WISKEY, BEER, WINE, SODA, TOBACCO, LUNCH and DANCING.

Strangely enough, the sign also reads: INDIANS ALLOWED—LAKOTA. I wonder aloud that this must be from a time when it was not taken for granted that an Indian was allowed to enter a bar. Kent says he vaguely remembers driving through here in the 1980s and seeing other words: NO INDIANS ALLOWED. I reflect how Native Americans coming by on this road every day must feel about such a derogatory statement and why they have not already taken down this sign a long time ago, even in its amended form.

The building looks as though the next South Dakota blizzard could topple it. But it has seen a lot of blizzards, hailstorms and extreme temperatures over the past century and survived all of it.

Longhorn Saloon with skulls dangling over the sign

Next to the saloon, looking just as old and authentic, is the Longhorn Store on Main Street. As the carved signs says, here you can buy GENERAL MERCHANDISE, LAKOTA ARTIFACTS and BEADWORK. Actually, you can BUY, SELL AND TRADE things. Another sign reads:

“ASHES TO ASHES—DUST TO DUST—
IF WE DON’T HAVE IT—IT ISN’T A MUST.”

I find that particularly this old sign features some of the old-time thinking, addressing potential clients in this partly biblical, partly humorous way.

Six old, rusty wagon wheels adorn the façade. There are also signs of modern day technology at this building: a window air conditioner sticking out of the front window and three pairs of light fixtures on top of the wooden roof that protects the front porch. We assume that these six lamps shine on the signs so that tourists can read them at night.

Longhorn Store

When I first see the Longhorn Saloon and Store I am not sure they really originate from 1906. I think they look more like a mock-up in order to attract tourists. But then I learn that these ramshackle buildings are indeed from the old times and have served their purpose all along.

In the old days, this was probably the only store in a fifty-mile radius and there was an actual need for it. Ranchers and town people would come to do their regular shopping here. Cowboys would hang out in the saloon next door. Nowadays these two buildings are more of a curiosity and a tourist attraction.

Also on Main Street is a long storefront. Windows and doors are boarded up. One of the businesses is called "Museum of Natural History." We don't know whether any of these stores or the museum will open during the summer months.

A Congregational church was built in 1920. This means the 155 inhabitants must have had a pastor among them. Were they all Congregationalists, and what about the other confessions—where did *they* hold their Sunday services? That the congregation could afford to build such a big structure is a sign of earlier prosperity in the town.

The building is still standing, but it is now called the *Tatanka Trading Post*. During the summer months, it probably serves as a snack bar. Some outside benches and a table let us assume that tourists sit there in the heat and drink cold beer and eat hot dogs.

Tatanka Trading Post,
formerly Congregational Church

The most solid structure of all the buildings in town is the jailhouse. It was built of river stones brought from the Cheyenne River seven miles away. This jail contains only two cells. The building is designed angular so that water and snow can flow down from the roof.

Jailhouse in Scenic

Besides the jailhouse, there are also two public jail cells located on Main Street. They are made of metal bars and open to wind, rain and onlookers. When I first see them, I mistake them for cattle cages. But Kent tells me he thinks they might have been designed to publically exhibit and humiliate people who had committed a crime. We can hardly imagine that's true. Unbelievable that such practices were still going on here in the early times of Scenic. But what else could those cages be used for?

Besides those old, ghostly buildings, there is also a quite normal looking post office in town. It is tiny and has only one employee, but still serves its purpose to support the surrounding ranches and homes.

Can you imagine working all by yourself out in the great nowhere in such a little post office? You would know all the patrons coming in from far and wide. You would be the hub not only of the ranching world of all of Scenic Township, which had a 2010 census population of 58 inhabitants, but also of parts of the reservation. People would come in to pick up their mail, buy stamps or mail a parcel and also to trade news from around the township.

U.S. Post Office in Scenic

Much bigger than the post office is the gas station. It is a functional building, maybe only a few decades old, and even open when we come here on a Saturday afternoon in February. The price for regular gas is the same as in Rapid City—$1.79 per gallon. This gas station looks as though it could be found in Rapid City or anywhere in the U.S.

Scenic gas station

In spite of a few businesses still functioning and about two or three houses still inhabited, Scenic is a ghost town. It looks more ghostly from year to year, with dilapidated shacks and houses falling into ruin.

One of many dilapidated houses in Scenic

But this story does not end in total ruins. As forlorn and run-down as it looks, Scenic might actually have a future, although still shrouded in mystery. Here is the story:

Twila Merrill, a famous rodeo girl from Manderson, started being involved with Scenic in the 1960s when she bought a bar and a house here. She ran the bar and a trucking business and traded horses. Slowly she acquired more and more of the town property until she owned most of it. But when she became too sick to continue, she put everything on the market. At first, she asked for three million dollars, but nobody bit. Who wants to pay such a horrendous sum to own a run-down town out in nowhere?

So Twila had to reduce the price. In July 2011, most of the 12-acre town and surrounding area—about 46 acres total—was listed for sale at $799,000. The sale included the post office, Longhorn Saloon, train depot, dance hall, bunkhouse, gas station, museum, and two stores. Suddenly, prospective buyers stepped forward from all over the world.

In August 2011, we were surprised to read in the Rapid City Journal that a Philippine church called *Iglesia ni Cristo* (Church of Christ), established in the Philippines in 1914, bought the property. "What are they going to do out there?" we wondered.

The church never disclosed why it acquired the property. Twila died in December 2014, in those last years of her life probably also wondering what was going to happen in Scenic. So far we have not seen any changes since the purchase, except for a banner at the entrance, welcoming bikers and tourists and announcing church services in the Community Hall on Thursdays and Sundays.

Church banner at the entrance to Scenic

The services have been held since July 2015 when an Iglesia ni Cristo minister moved to the area. Ten to fifteen congregants who live nearby or even as far away as Sturgis attend them.

What looks like a tiny group in Scenic is backed by far greater numbers across the world. In the Philippines, Iglesia ni Cristo is the second largest Christian church after the Catholic Church and worldwide has about 2.25 million members and over 6,000 congregations .

Community Hall were the services take place

Since 1914, the church has been steadily spreading west since it was founded in the Philippines by Felix Manalo, a former minister of the Seventh-Day Adventist Church who experienced what he claimed to be a call similar to those of ancient prophets. He died in 1963. Iglesia ni Cristo is focused on the end times, believes Manalo was a prophet and considers the Catholic Church apostate.

Here in Scenic, Iglesia ni Cristo has not filed any building permits or stated development plans for the land or filed for tax-exempt status. So far, there has been no activity to hint at what is to come. I can imagine that the lack of information surrounding the sale has some neighbors uneasy and rumors are circulating among them. What happens next is not known publicly.

The real estate manager who finalized the sale said the property will be cleaned of dilapidated buildings and overgrown brush, but he said the saloon and other boarded-up buildings still standing along Main Street will stay. Although he couldn't give specifics, we think there must be some secret plans because nobody, not even a big church organization, would spend hundreds of thousands of dollars on property without having a plan in mind of what to do with it. Whenever we travel to the Badlands, we'll keep an eye out for any new development in Scenic.

Eroding Beauty

At the end of February, we enjoy an extremely good day in the Badlands. From Scenic, we drive on a dirt road south toward Sheep Mountain Table. At first we think the mountains around us look scraggy, gray and barren, almost boring.

On the way to Sheep Mountain Table

But when we look closer, we see something unexpected—a huge field of mushrooms made of stone. In this super dry climate, you would of course not find real mushrooms. The strangest formations are rising from the ground. Some of them are several feet tall, others smaller. They come in all sizes and shapes, and we see thousands of them. Other such structures stick out sideways from the base rock like long noses. Still others have partially tumbled down and are now resting on the steep slopes as though they could come crashing down like an avalanche at any moment. These strange sculptures are sitting on rock that looks like solidified clay.

Mushroom-like rock formations

Long noses sticking out and tumbled-down rocks

We drive about ten miles until we reach a plateau and can't drive any farther because the only road is so washed out that we can't take it with our car. We have come to a very steep precipice. It drops 340 feet straight down from where we stand. Better not stumble or take any false steps here! The rock is very brittle and looks like dried mud held together by some tired winter grass.

View down into a steep valley from Sheep Mountain Table

Can you imagine walking through these crevices, only to reach another crevice and then another one? It must be very easy to get lost in this maze of steep canyon walls. From time to time, we read in the newspaper that a hiker lost his way in the Badlands or that he got dehydrated. We have also heard of people being bitten by rattlesnakes. There is an abundance of rattlesnakes in these crevices.

What else could we find here? There are mule deer, bighorn sheep, pronghorn, coyotes and even bison living here. Prairie dogs live in the less steep places. If we went into these crevices, would we find skeletons of animals or humans who died here, eaten and gnawed on by coyotes and vultures and then left to bleach in the sun? This place evokes that feeling.

Golden eagles and prairie falcons nest on the steep cliffs. Cliff swallows build their mud nests in sheltered regions of the slopes. Cedar waxwings eat juniper berries from the bushes that can be found here and there. All in all, sixty-seven bird species are known to nest here.

A hole just big enough for a man to slide through opens down into nowhere. Who made this hole and why? Nobody in his clear mind would want to climb down these eroded slopes into the bottomless chasm. Or is this hole itself, so smoothly and evenly shaped, also the result of erosion?

Big hole at the brink of the gaping abyss

Standing in the grass on top of the cliffs, we realize that they have many more holes in them. Not knowing it, we might stand exactly on top of one of these cavities or caves. When did they form, and how long have they been there? Maybe they cracked apart hundreds or thousands of years ago. Or did a heavy rain wash them out just this winter? We don't know, but it feels funny to look at them while standing not far away on the same cliff.

Holes underneath the cliff on which we are standing

From the first plateau on, we hike farther on a jeep road up to Sheep Mountain Table. Reddish-brown grasses, yucca plants and some lone juniper bushes grow along our trail. We see pronghorn tracks in the sand and some far-away buttes standing in the endless ocean of dried grass and mullein stalks from last year.

Hiking is great fun here because of the wonderful, flowerlike fragrance in the air. We don't know where it comes from. Nothing is in bloom now, at the end of February. It can't come from the junipers because we are familiar with the fragrance of juniper, and that's not what this heavenly, sublime scent is like. I guess it will remain a mystery forever.

Grasses, yucca plants, mullein stalks, a lone juniper bush and rock butte in the distance

When we reach another, higher plateau we see our car far away, on top of the cliff where we first looked out into the ragged landscape. It is almost frightening to see how close to the 340-foot abyss we parked. From our new standpoint, we now look out into even more layers and layers of rugged mountains.

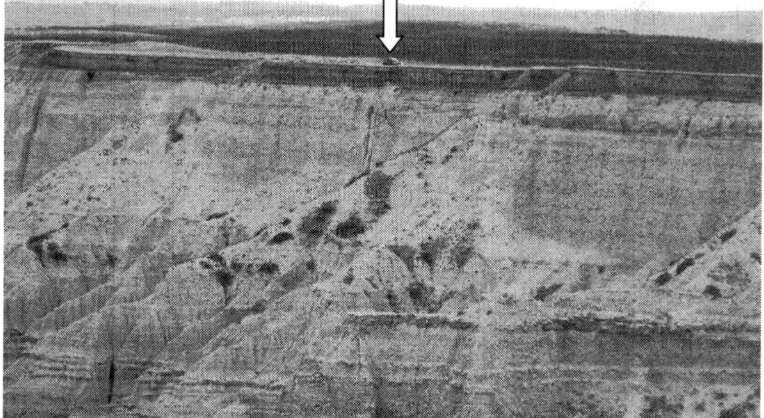

Can you spot our car on top of the cliff?

This photo reminds me of Caspar David Friedrich's oil painting of Chalk Cliffs on the island of Rügen, Germany

Eroded spires with the Black Hills and Black Elk Peak on the horizon

Far away in the distance, we see the outline of the Black Hills in a haze and can even make out Black Elk Peak, the highest mountain. Amazing that we can see the Black Hills from here, forty miles away.

We wonder what these ghostly spires around here looked like thousands or even millions of years ago. How and when did they form? As you can see on the above photos, the Badlands were deposited in layers, some darker, some lighter. The oldest formations are at the bottom, the youngest at the top.

This is sedimentary rock, consisting of sand, silt and clay. Each layer of sediment formed over aeons, with the first layer accumulating seventy-five million years ago, and the top layer capping off about twenty-six million years ago. Scientists have names for the different periods of time when these sediments were deposited. They even know what climatic conditions caused which sediments to be accumulated.

The lowest layer was deposited when a huge inland sea stretched across what is now the Great Plains. Black mud slowly formed at the bottom of the sea and then hardened into shale. This layer is called Pierre Shale and it still contains fossils of sea reptiles, clams and ammonites.

The next layer was formed when the Black Hills lifted up and the sea drained away. Ancient rivers crossed the plains. Each time the rivers flooded, they deposited a new layer of mud on the plains.

This whole region lay closer to the equator then and was much more humid. During this time, alligators and the three-toed horse lived here in a subtropical forest. How the climate and precipitation have changed since that time!

Eventually it became dryer and cooler, and open savannah replaced the forests. A big event during that period of the development of the Badlands was a volcanic eruption further west that sent thick clouds of volcanic ash to this region. In many places, the ash now forms a gray band around the rugged peaks.

When layer upon layer became deposited on the plains, why doesn't this landscape just look like one big cake instead of sharply defined buttes, pinnacles, gullies and ridges? The answer is erosion. Beginning a half million years ago, the big cake was gradually sliced by wind, water, ice and sun. Rivers from the Black Hills cut through the layers of rock and carried countless tons of sediment with them. It is amazing for us to see what erosion can do. The imagination plays along, turning the strangest shapes into mushrooms, pillars and sandcastles.

Formations like sandcastles

I asked the Badlands Information Center at what rate erosion is taking place. They say erosion varies greatly throughout the formations with several inches per year where active landslides are taking place to only a few millimeters where resistant sandstone is dominant. All in all, the Badlands are a relatively short-lived phenomenon and might be entirely gone in about 500,000 years. If they started out about 500,000 years ago and will be totally gone in another 500,000 years—one million years altogether—that's not a long life span for something as timeless as the fantastic shapes of the Badlands!

These eroding beauties have such an otherworldly, eternal appearance that it is hard to believe that, geologically speaking, they are as ephemeral as clouds. Just a blink of an eye for the earth, and they're gone. Only one million years, but for us, this is an eternity in itself.

On one of the lower levels, we see a strange phenomenon that at first startles me. On a rock ledge all along the formation, we see structures that look like human dwellings. We can make out windows and doors. Are these ancient houses? Is this an adobe village of cliff dwellers, abandoned long ago? But no, these are just more fantastic shapes. Erosion exposed the ledge of harder rock, and erosion created the holes in the softer rock underneath.

Rock formation resembling ancient houses

Seeing these holes resembling windows makes us wonder, though, whether some outlaws fled into this area and lived here for a while in a cave. What would they have lived on? Maybe they could have trapped rattlesnakes or prairie dogs and even bigger mammals and then roasted them over a fire hidden in the cave.

We don't think the outlaws could have ridden a horse because, although this is such a remote and expansive area, it is also very open and the tracks of the hooves would have been visible in the sand and gravel for miles.

We look down into areas that might flood when a rare torrential downpour hits the Badlands. Is this one of the ancient river beds, now still visible, that I talked about earlier? It would be quite an experience to see this river flow after strong rains.

River bed in the canyon below

When checking the map, we find out that there is yet a third, higher plateau of the Sheep Mountain Table above our current position. We have walked enough today and have to leave exploration of the third plateau for a different day.

In consulting the map, we also realize how big the Badlands are—244,000 acres just for the Badlands National Park, and the Badlands extend much beyond that park. How did the early settlers deal with this huge expanse? Did they find their way through it or did they know how to travel around it?

We also see several dirt roads on the map, most of them ending nowhere. But they must have been created for some reason. Is it possible that there are places where people live among these spires and folds of the Badlands?

After seeing all these natural wonders, we ask ourselves what is coming next? Another volcanic explosion that will deposit more ash on this region, or global warming creating another subtropical environment? But, as I said before, for us the Badlands already represent eternity. We are not able to think beyond that.

Powerless

Black Hills weather is unpredictable. It changes quickly from one extreme to the next. On a Monday night in August, we have a hailstorm. The hailstones, measuring one inch in diameter, hit our house like ping-pong balls stuffed with cement. These hard ice bullets pelt the roof and windows with such power it seems they are going to smash everything to pieces. A flood of rain follows the bombardment. This is not regular rain as we have almost every day in Germany, but more like a wall of water coming down sideways, hitting the dried-out ground hard.

When the rain is over we see a huge thunderstorm to the south. If this were a regular thunderstorm you would see some lightning here and there and hear the thunderclap a few seconds after each flash; you would hear water rushing down from the sky, and usually after twenty or thirty minutes the whole spectacle would be over and the air clear and fresh.

No, our thunderstorm on Monday night is different! It spreads out over the whole southern horizon and consists of constant lightning, zigzagging from one side to the other. Never before have I seen lightning like this going on and on, never pausing for more than two seconds. We do not hear any thunder, but watch these extreme strikes for over an hour. They are taking on different shapes; sometimes they are almost circular, at other times going straight down into the ground, then long drawn out and parallel to the horizon. We assume that what we see is heat lightning.

The following day, Tuesday, is hot again. During the 98°F heat in the afternoon, another thunderstorm is gathering. But it does not unload any rain on our region. We just see it coming, sailing by us and disappearing into the eastern sky. So we are able to take a walk in the evening sun. For once, the weather looks harmless, and when we go to bed around ten o'clock we have no hunch of what is coming.

Half an hour later, when we are sound asleep, a huge concussion wave hits the southern wall of our house with a roaring sound. Has an asteroid struck the earth? We jump out of bed to see what is going on. This time, there is no rain, no hail, no lightning and no thunder. It is just an enormous wind that is roaring with unimaginable strength. Actually, it is a real storm, like a hurricane. And here it comes again, racing against our house like a truck. With full force, it bangs against the walls. And again and again, each time whirling up more power it seems. Will it break the windows? Carry off the roof? Take the walls down?

No, but the power goes off—not only in our house, but in the whole settlement. It is quite dark now without any street lights. "Well, this can happen in a storm of this strength," we think. "Probably the power will be restored in a few minutes."

As suddenly as the hurricane came, it subsides. It has lasted for only twenty minutes or so, and quietness has come back to our neighborhood. It is eerie, but also kind of nice to have the streets so dark.

The only thing I miss is the overhead fan in the bedroom. During hot nights like this, it helps me maintain a comfortable temperature for sleeping. Tonight's storm has not cooled down the air a bit. We sleep anyway, but are having a rough night. In my sleep, I am still waiting for that fan to come on again because I expect the power certainly to be restored during the night.

The next morning, after waking up from this hot and restless sleep, my first thought is: "What was this powerful monster that hit our house last night? It must have been nothing but a bad dream. But why then is it so hot in the bedroom?" My next thought is with the fan, and I look upward. No, it is not running. Still no power in the house! A hot day of 95° is predicted. Our AC is not working. How will we be able to withstand such temperatures in the house all day long? Other inconveniences cross my mind. Without power, we won't be able to reach the Internet, which means we can't translate or proofread. I can't cook the morning porridge or boil the morning tea, can't cook lunch, can't vacuum, can't skype with my daughter or receive e-mails.

Looking out of the window, I see about fifty apples that were supposed to ripen on the tree lying on the grass below. Well, I will have to cut them up and make applesauce when the power is back.

About fifty unripe apples under the tree

We look at each other and ask ourselves: "What are we going to do today? And what are we going to eat?" First of all, we try to take a shower. To our amazement, the hot water comes out of the faucet just fine. We know it is heated by gas, but assumed that it needed an electronic sensor and spark to come on, but this does not seem to be required.

Next point: breakfast. Our fridge is filled with good food, but we are afraid that opening the door would let warm air into it, and we don't want the food inside to be spoiled. So we drink cold water, eat a banana, some nuts and rice cakes, and then we walk the neighborhood in order to find out what the situation is.

Some trees were topped by the storm and their crowns lie on the ground. Many twigs, branches and leaves are down. So far, it looks just like the aftermath of a strong thunderstorm and nothing out of the normal.

But when we reach the northern border of our settlement, we see the reason for the power outage—thirteen power poles lying on the ground. These are huge poles, eighty-five feet long. The storm must have snapped the heavy poles off like toothpicks. They took the power lines down with them. The whole northern road is blocked off. The people in these houses cannot take their cars out of the garages in order to drive to work.

Heavy power poles broken off like toothpicks

Emergency trucks lined up to help;
in the background people rushing to bring their meat to safety

A TV crew is at the scene taking photos and interviewing homeowners. There is a lot going on here today in this usually quiet neighborhood. People are talking to each other. I see people with coolers and bags heavy with frozen meat rushing down the street to their car. "Where are you taking the meat?" I ask them. "To our friends' freezer in town," they say. "We are afraid that all our meat will go to waste if the outage lasts much longer."

Power lines lying on the ground after the big storm

New power poles, 45 feet long, for the emergency line

Several trucks carrying cranes are lined up to help. One of them carries thirteen new poles. But these are shorter than the original poles, only 45 feet long. "Are you going to erect an emergency line with these shorter poles?" we ask a worker. "Yes, we hope to have some emergency power back up by tonight," he explains.

When we return to our house, we hear a loud generator noise. A vehicle from a broadband company stands in front of our house. This company has a gas-powered generator in their cable box in our front yard and came to start it up. This helps the customers in the neighborhood get signal, but we're not sure what good that will do as customers have no power to turn on their devices. We will have to endure this obnoxious noise as long as the power outage lasts.

It's not only the AC, the computers, phone and fridge that are not working, but we are surprised to realize that every nook and corner of the house relies on electricity in some way. Many times throughout the day we catch ourselves automatically flipping the light switch of a closet or trying to turn on different gadgets in the house before realizing that all of this is out of commission today. Amazing how powerless we are without power!

To escape the heat in the house and the noise from the front yard, we decide to make the best of the situation and go swimming. But how do we get the car out of our house without the electric garage door opener? For the first time in nine years, we pull at the emergency cord that allows a person to open the garage door manually, and it works. What a luxury to go swimming on a weekday before noon! We are the only ones at the beach and enjoy our swim immensely.

On the way home, we buy a 20-pound bag of ice cubes to fill into little plastic containers which I then stick into the fridge and freezer so that our food will stay cool longer. Kent drives to the library in town in order to work on his translation project. In the meantime, I am almost getting used to the fact that we don't have electricity. It's so quiet at home when no washer or other gadgets are running. I start writing this story by hand, an activity I have not done for many years.

At 5:50 p.m., nineteen hours after the power went out, I hear an unexpected noise in my office. The telephone has come back on! I run to the bedroom and see that the fan is running again! Downstairs I hear the fridge working. That's good news. I am able to write and receive e-mails and can notify Kent to return home.

We are very fortunate to be among the first to have electricity again. As I hear the next morning from the workers, they worked until 11:30 p.m. and many other households did not have their power back until that late hour.

The next morning, the first page of our newspaper carries a story on the unconventional storm. They call it a "rare heat burst" which usually occurs at night when a thunderstorm "decays." It descends from high in the atmosphere, maybe from 30,000 feet to the ground, suddenly bringing extremely high winds and dry air. Heat bursts can occur anywhere in the world, but are mostly observed here in the Great Plains. They happen across South Dakota a few times each summer.

In our case, this weather phenomenon was a very localized event, and it occurred primarily in our neighborhood. The speed of the storm was about 100 miles per hour, which explains why thirteen power poles were knocked down along a single row about a mile long. The work crew from the utility company told us they had never seen anything like it, as the poles that snapped were new and strong.

Fortunately the storm raced from south to north, so the poles fell northwards, away from the houses on the developed side of the street. "Couldn't the falling poles have caused a terrible fire?" I asked one of the workers. "No, the power was knocked out before they all fell—the poles were not under load," he explained. About 400 people were without power for nineteen to twenty-five hours.

It would be good if my story could end here. But the turbulent weather conditions this August bring us even more unexpected weather. Only three days after the heat burst, we have a regular thunderstorm with heavy winds and rain, this time coming from the north.

When we walk our neighborhood the next day, we see that the new poles with the emergency power lines are tilted about 10 degrees to the south, toward the houses. Nobody seems to mind, but it does look dangerous to us, or would you like to live in a house with a power pole leaning toward you like this?

Temporary poles leaning about 10 degrees toward the houses

The good news is that the workmen have started erecting taller, stronger power poles right next to the tilted 45-foot poles. The new ones are 85 to 100 feet tall. In lower spots, 90- or 100-foot poles are installed, in higher spots the 85-foot ones. The workers also tell us now that the temporary poles were installed in this tilted manner so that they would not interfere with the new permanent poles.

We can only hope that the new poles are deep enough in the ground and strong enough to withstand the coming thunderstorms and heat bursts. And that the power will be transferred to them before the next thunderstorm knocks over the small poles!

Stronger power poles next to the small emergency poles

Are we done with the severe weather conditions yet? Our neighborhood seems to be safe for now. But the unsettled atmosphere has more in store for Rapid City. A few days later, we hear in the news that an airplane on a flight from Boston to Sacramento had to make an emergency landing in Rapid City.

Twenty-four people were taken to the hospital after the airplane encountered severe turbulence at a very high altitude. The plane had suddenly dropped 500 feet, lifting passengers out of their seats and slamming them into the ceiling or overhead compartments. Fortunately they suffered only minor injuries, but it was enough to make the national news.

Two weeks after the big heat burst, it is almost forgotten, except for the scarily slanted 45-foot power poles that still carry our electricity. "How long will it take to transfer those power lines to the big poles?" we ask each other every time we go by. "Hopefully we will be notified of any power outage before the workers come again to fix this."

So we think. But nineteen days after the big event, we are out of power again at 9:00 o'clock on a Monday morning. We have not received any notification and have no idea how long it will take this time. We call the power company, but they can only tell us that 290 households are without power and that they have no idea how long this will last. Is it time to buy more ice cubes? We postpone that a little, and as it's a hot day again, we go swimming once more.

Five hours later at the lake, we receive a phone call from the power company that we will be out of power on Monday morning for about five hours, starting at 9:00 o'clock. That warning is a bit late, I'd say! We expect the power has been restored and drive home. Upon our arrival, we are happy to watch our garage door open as we press the button. Inside we find the fridge and all the other appliances running again.

Two weeks have passed, the weather has adopted a cooler, pre-autumn mood and I am just putting this story into final shape. This was a jacket day, perhaps with a hint of winter to come. The heat of August past, I feel confident that no further meteorological events will bear reporting this month.

And yet, as though to provide punctuation for this story, the sky suddenly blackens and barrages the house with BB-sized hail. Not destructive, but just enough for the sky to tell us, "Don't become complacent!" Who would have predicted such hail from a cold sky? But that's enough. If I keep writing about the quirks of Black Hills weather, this story will never end.

Fountain of Youth in South Dakota

I never thought it would be possible to swim outdoors in South Dakota in the middle of September. After our swim in Pactola Lake on August 29, I assumed this was probably the last swim of the year because the water was quite cold at about 68°F. The nights got colder after that, with temperatures in the forties and fifties.

But South Dakota never fails to surprise us. In rolling grasslands just south of the higher Black Hills, we find the nicest swimming hole you could ever ask for. Invisible from the road, only word of mouth invites you to stop. When we visit Cascade Falls in Alabough Canyon nine miles southwest of Hot Springs on September 17, we park at the road, as the gravel parking lot is already cordoned off for the winter.

We walk down to Cascade Creek and dip our hands into the water. Wow, it is still acceptable for swimming. Cascade Falls is fed year-round by a warm spring with a water temperature of 67°F.

Upper part of Cascade Falls

We wade toward the upper part of the Falls and, along the banks, admire the lush vegetation and the last wildflowers of the year—golden glow, goldenrod, white aster and sunflowers. Because of the warm water, even rare plants can be seen here—the stream orchid, maidenhair fern, tulip gentian and spikerush. These four plants cannot be found anywhere else in South Dakota—only here in this environment at Cascade Creek and its tributaries.

Maidenhair fern along the banks, hanging down to the water

Over the lower part of the Falls, we slide down into a natural pool where swimming in the blue water is fantastic. The pool is so deep that in most of it we cannot touch the ground. And yet, the water is so clear that we can see to the bottom.

Originally the water here was dammed by beavers, and later on, this natural dam filled up with calcite and became permanent. This swimming hole has been used by settlers since the 1880s. And they were not the first ones to discover the fun of swimming in this relatively warm water. Native Americans have come to this creek for ages.

Lower part of Cascade Falls with pool

Where does the clear, warm water of Cascade Creek come from? It originates from six artesian springs about two miles higher up in Alabough Canyon. One of them, called "Cascade Springs," gushes out 2,000 gallons of warm water per minute. This is one of the most pristine waters in South Dakota and supports a uniquely warm riverine ecosystem. A round stone basin contains this spring.

Cascade Springs form Cascade Creek

In the 1880s, some cowboys driving their cattle over the nearby hills reported seeing the eruption of a mud geyser on one of the slopes. I bet they were scared because they had not been aware of volcanic activity in this region. It somehow explains why the surface waters are warmer here than in the rest of South Dakota.

In the late 1880s, a white man, hunting in this region, discovered the springs and had the idea to capitalize on them. He contacted a banker, and from then on, this region saw quite a boom, especially since a rumor was going around that the mineral water had medicinal value.

The list of chronic diseases that this water could cure became longer and longer. It would help with problems of the liver, the gastrointestinal and urinary tracts, rheumatism, gout, scrofula, malaria, constipation, neuralgia, syphilis, gynecological disorders and more.

I don't know how true these claims were, but people came in flocks and started up their residences and businesses. Rich businessmen from Chicago saw their chance here to become even richer. They invested in the town of Cascade which was founded in the 1880s between Cascade Springs and the Falls. They had great aspirations to make it a thriving spa destination, where guests would drink the Cascade water and bathe in it in the belief that it would cure in a magical way.

The wetland along Cascade Creek was filled to create the town on this ground. Thirty-six city blocks were laid out, and construction of many wooden and several big sandstone buildings started. The residents were proud of their half-mile boardwalk which went through town.

A four story, hundred-room hotel was built, along with a bath house and sanatorium. Even a bowling alley sprang up that could be entered through a drive-in livery stable. A grocery store, dance hall and saloon were necessary, too. In 1892, Cascade had almost 400 residents, about fifty businesses, a bank and a post office. Of course a newspaper was also published, with the name *Cascade Geyser*.

Many people dumped all they had into this dream of a prosperous town built around a natural fountain of youth. And they did not just dream, but were very industrious, digging an irrigation system by hand all the way to the Cheyenne River—about a thousand yards away. Apple trees were planted and beautiful orchards created.

How were all these people connected to the outside world? They took the stagecoach to Hot Springs, which was linked to the surrounding towns by railroad. It all sounded like heaven had descended on earth and life could be so perfect and healthy here. Some residents even envisioned creating a 60-acre lake, but this plan never came to pass.

Many other dreams and hopes of the inhabitants of Cascade also got shattered quickly. Some say the decline of Cascade was due to the investors in Chicago losing interest in this frontier health resort. Or was it the competition with nearby Hot Springs that destroyed the hopes for Cascade? Others say the fact that railroad construction never reached the town smashed all hopes for a glowing future. Maybe all three of these reasons were true?

Or did the mineral waters not fulfill the promises of curing all the ailments listed in the town's advertising brochures? Was this the reason why people, after all this boom and buzz, turned their backs on Cascade? The truth is that, by 1900, not much was left of Cascade. It consisted only of a post office, with no more than twenty-five people remaining. Most of them also left shortly after.

In 1907, another incident happened that indicated volcanic activity. All of a sudden, the springs turned red. I can only guess that some underground activity made the iron content of the rocks leach upwards into the water. But at this point, most of the people had left anyway, and the red water could not damage the reputation of the health spa any more than had already occurred.

What happened to all the buildings, especially those luxurious sandstone constructions? The wooden structures decayed over time and had to be removed. The sanatorium and hotel, which had actually never been in use, were also removed. Their big sandstone blocks were dismantled and hauled to Hot Springs for the construction of the hospital and other buildings in that bigger, thriving town.

Only one building still stands today, and that is the Allen Bank. It probably never served as a bank, but was converted into livable space early on by dividing the big bank room on the ground floor into three rooms. At first, there was no running water in this building.

Old bank building in Cascade, once owned by the Keith family, now by Cindy Reed and her husband Marc Lamphere

The only people who stayed in town when everybody left lived in this picturesque bank building. It was a couple, named J.G. and J.H. Keith, with their three children. They were founders of Cascade and remained here for decades after everyone else had given up and left town.

Most of the land around the former town was owned by the Keith family. Nowadays there is still an old wrought-iron sign in the wilderness near Cascade Springs that says: “J.H. Keith Park.”

The Keith heirs eventually donated Cascade Springs and Falls to the Forest Service, in whose possession they still are. I think it is great that they gave their land with such special features to the public. If they had not done it, we would not have been able to access the swimming hole of Cascade Falls today.

The old Allen Bank is still in good shape, thanks to Cindy Reed and her husband Marc Lamphere. They have lived here since 1976, which means for quite a long time! When they moved in, the building was in desolate shape. It had been vandalized, everything had been taken away from the inside of it and the whole place had been trashed. Moreover, a tree had crashed into the roof and damaged it severely.

Besides all the fixing-up Cindy and Marc needed to do, they also replaced the lead pipes, installed electricity and renewed the plumbing. It was a lot of work, but they seem to be happy to live here, and she says the warm mineral waters have done them good—although being older now, they don’t have any complaints.

The wetlands along the creek that once were filled up to create the town have come back on their own. A new, but shorter boardwalk has been created through them. The foundation of one of the old sandstone homes can still be seen in the tall grass. The irrigation system still exists and is now used to grow alfalfa.

We enjoyed our day and especially the swimming here today, but we don’t think we will come here in the dead of winter to swim. The air would be too cold, and even 67^0F water temperature could not make up for wind and frosty air.

Also, we suspect the temperature drops and rises somewhat depending on the ambient temperature. I wouldn't expect it to be 67 degrees at the Falls when there's ice and snow around. At least it would be worth checking out some winter when we are in the area.

There are other options for swimming in this region during the winter months. In Hot Springs, only nine miles away, is a natural indoor pool called Evans Plunge. The water temperature is 87^{0}F year-round. No heating of the water is needed, no chlorine is used. Swimming there is very comfortable.

I will have to tell you about this pool, the town of Hot Springs and the drinkable mineral water flowing out of the rock canyon wall at Kidney Springs in one of my future books.

Also by the author:

In Search of Secret South Dakota

Finding Poet's Table—and Other Black Hills Gems

South Dakota Firsthand: Through the Eyes of German Immigrant Edith-Maria Redlin

Wahres aus dem Wilden Westen, by John Hafnor
(German translation by Edith-Maria Redlin)

17132542R00073

Printed in Poland
by Amazon Fulfillment
Poland Sp. z o.o., Wrocław